14 POP HITS
FOR BIG-NOTE PIANO

HEY, SOUL SISTER

I KNEW YOU WERE TROUBLE — TAYLOR SWIFT

SOME NIGHTS — FUN

ROLLING IN THE DEEP — ADELE

STRONGER (WHAT DOESN'T KILL YOU) — KELLY CLARKSON

JUST THE WAY YOU ARE — BRUNO MARS

ISBN 978-1-4803-4326-9

HAL•LEONARD®
CORPORATION
7777 W. BLUEMOUND RD. P.O. BOX 13819 MILWAUKEE, WI 53213

Visit Hal Leonard Online at
www.halleonard.com

HEY, SOUL SISTER

Words and Music by PAT MONAHAN,
ESPEN LIND and AMUND BJORKLAND

need. Some gang - sta, I'm so thug, you're the on - ly one I'm dream - ing of. You

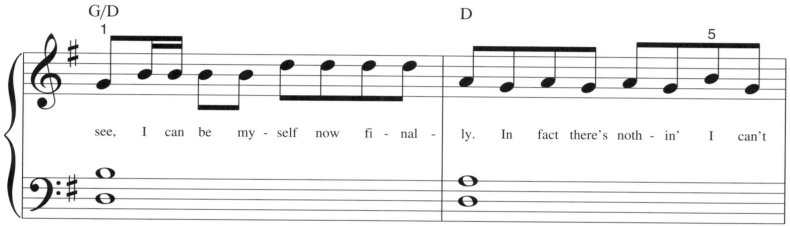

see, I can be my - self now fi - nal - ly. In fact there's noth - in' I can't

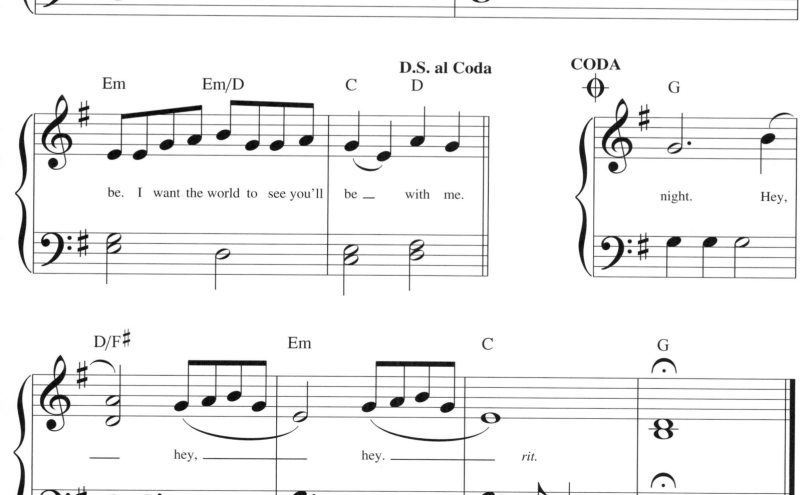

be. I want the world to see you'll be — with me.

D.S. al Coda

CODA

night. Hey,

hey, _____ hey. _____ rit.

HOME

Words and Music by GREG HOLDEN
and DREW PEARSON

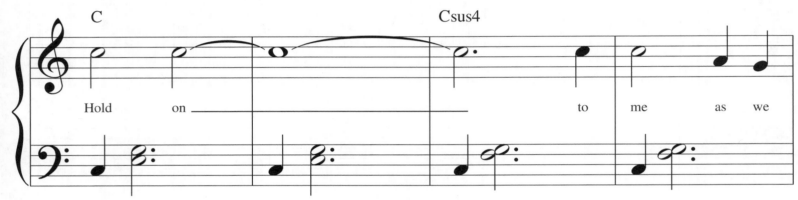

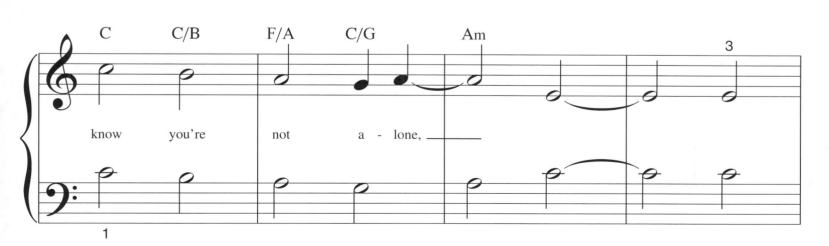

'cause I'm gon - na make this place your _____ home.

Set - tle down, _____

it - 'll all be clear.

Don't pay no

Csus4   C

mind   to   the   de - mons; they   fill   you   with   fear.

Csus4   A7

Trou - ble,   it

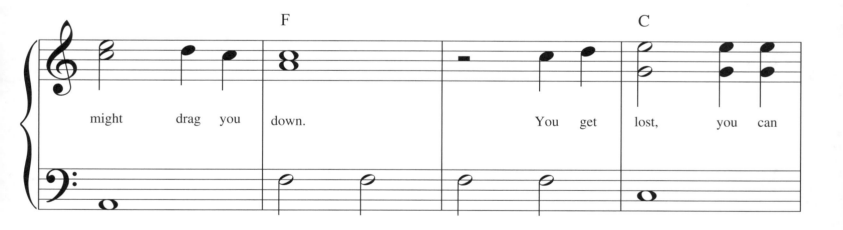

F   C

might   drag   you   down.   You   get   lost,   you   can

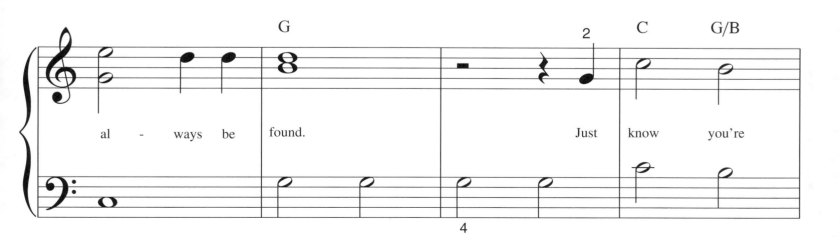

G   C   G/B

al - ways   be   found.   Just   know   you're

4

not a - lone,   'cause I'm gon - na

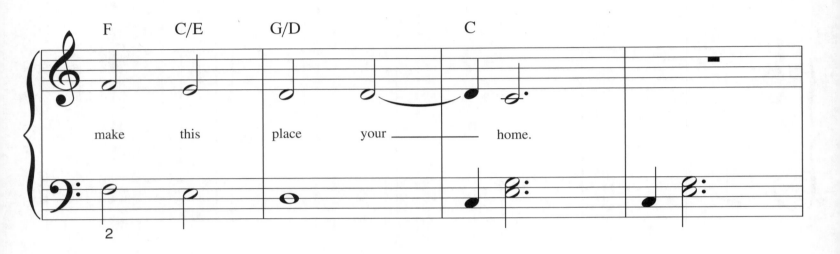

make   this   place   your _____ home.

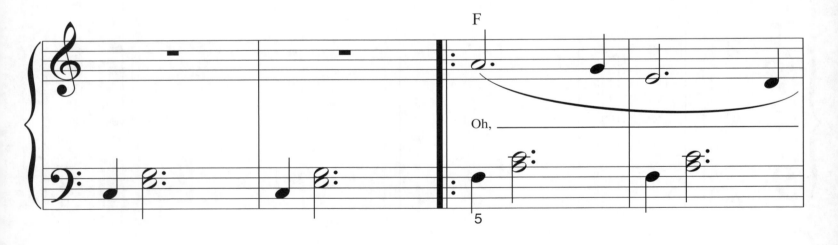

Oh, _____

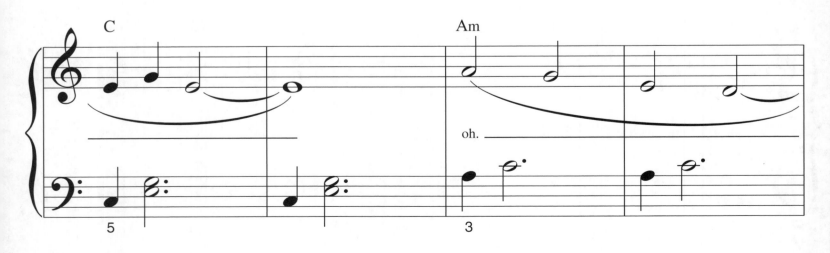

oh. _____

JAR OF HEARTS

Words and Music by BARRETT YERETSIAN,
CHRISTINA PERRI and DREW LAWRENCE

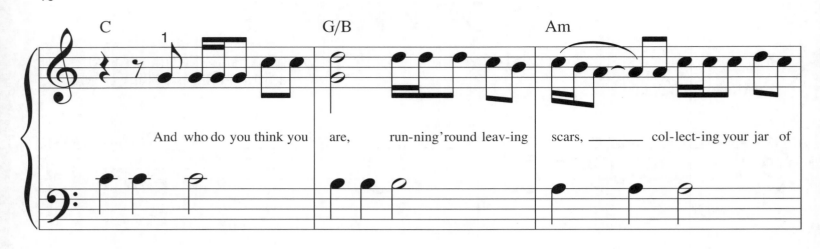

And who do you think you are, run-ning 'round leav-ing scars, _____ col-lect-ing your jar of

hearts and tear-ing love a-part? You're gon-na catch a cold _____ from the ice in-side your

To Coda

soul. _____ So don't come back for me. Who do you think you are?

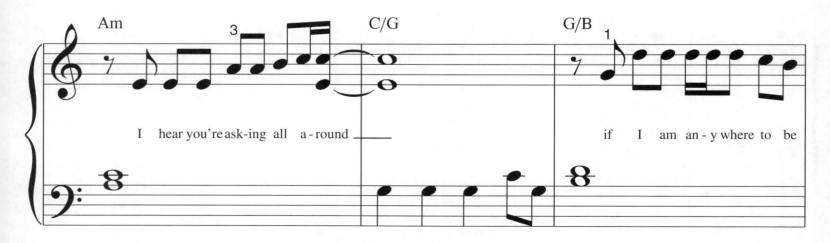

I hear you're ask-ing all a-round _____ if I am an-y where to be

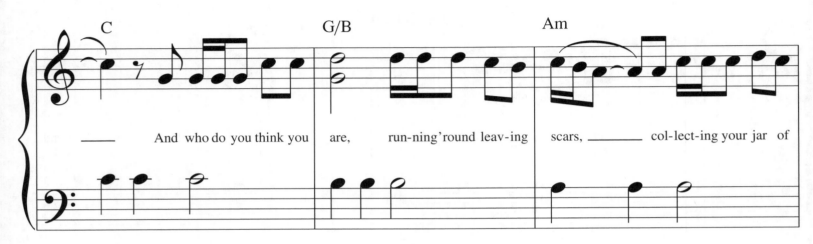

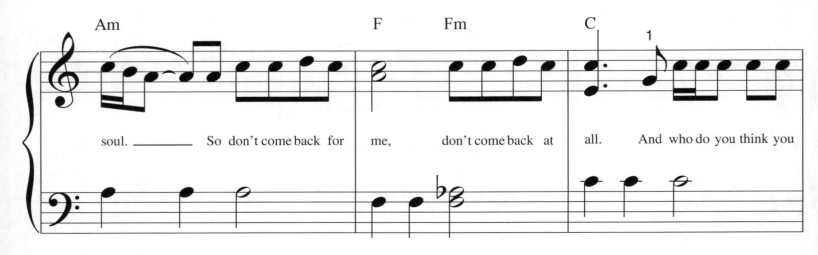

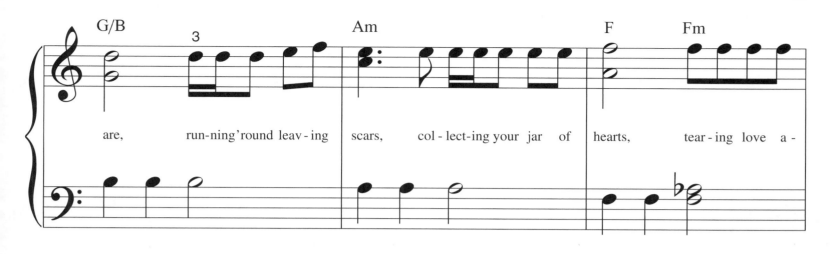

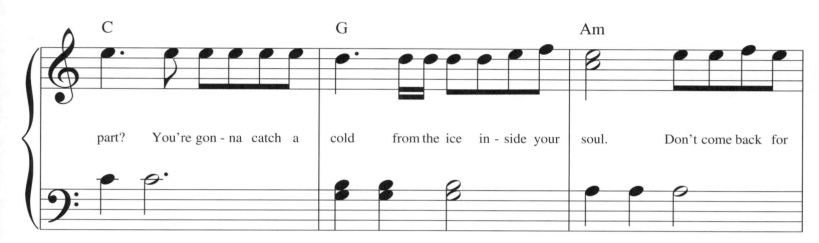

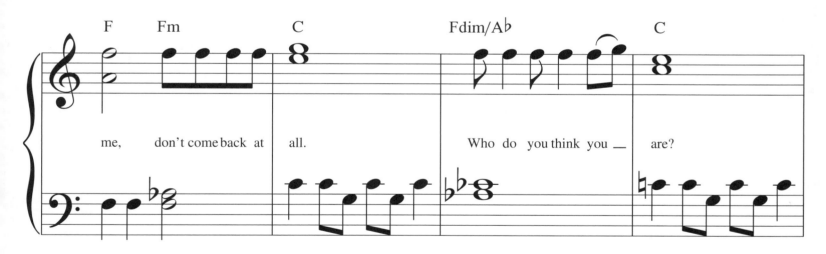

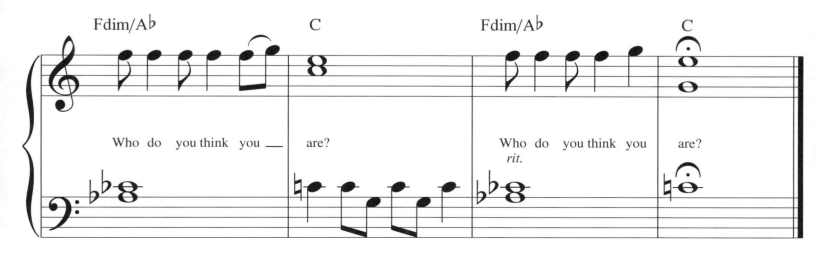

I KNEW YOU WERE TROUBLE.

Words and Music by TAYLOR SWIFT,
SHELLBACK and MAX MARTIN

Moderately fast

Once up-on a time a few mis-takes a-go, I was in your sights,
No a-pol-o-gies, he'll nev-er see you cry. Pre-tends he does-n't know that

you got me a-lone. You found _____ me, you found _____ me, you
he's the rea-son why you're drown - ing, you're drown - ing, you're

found _____ me, ee, ee, ee, ee. I guess you did-n't care and I
drown - ing, ing, ing, ing, ing. And I heard you moved on from

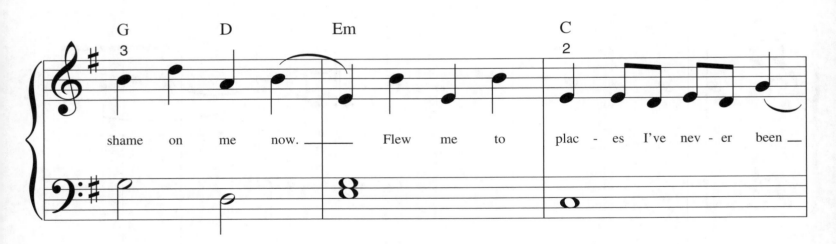

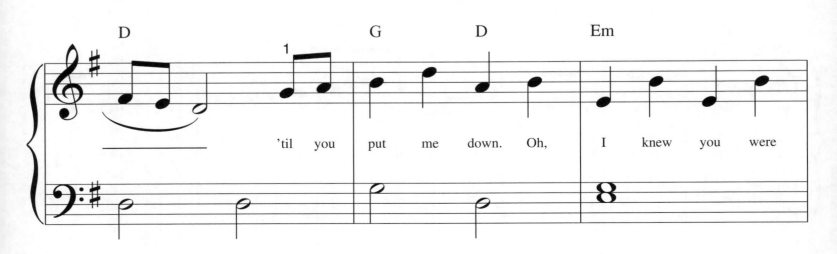

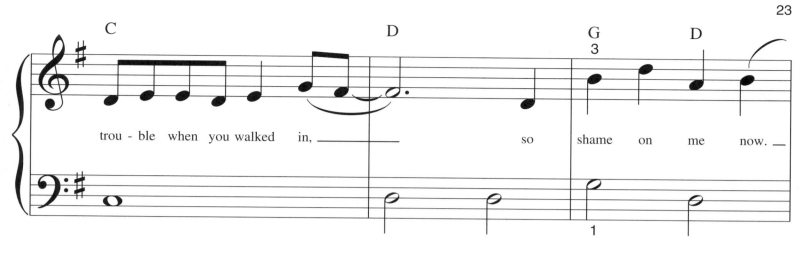

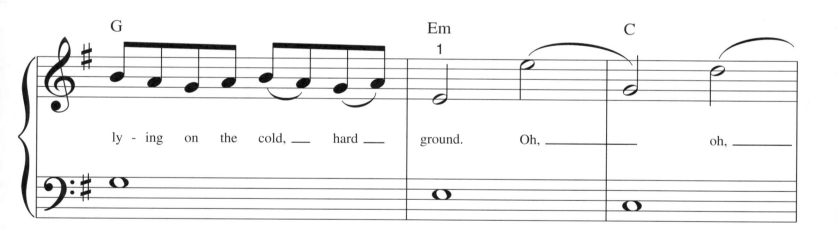

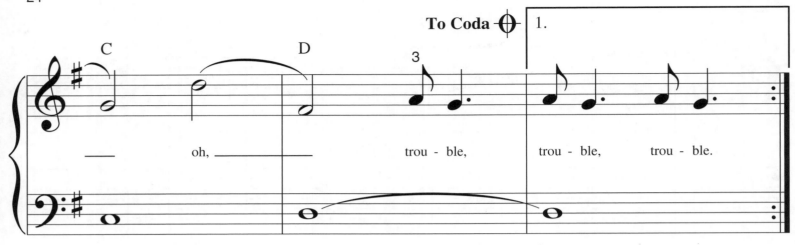

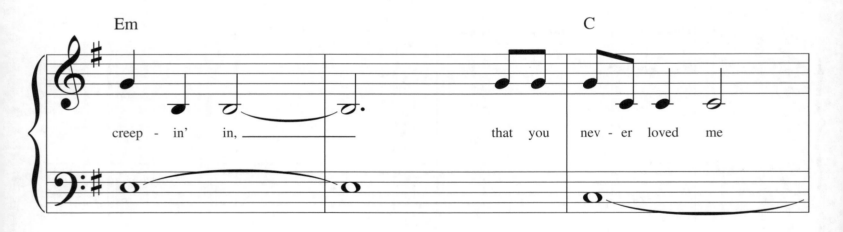

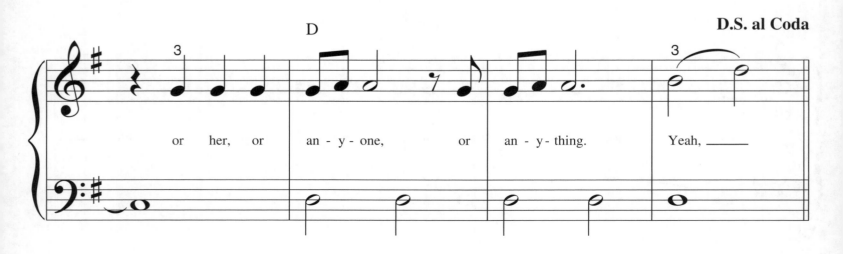

CODA

trou - ble,   trou - ble.   I   knew   you   were

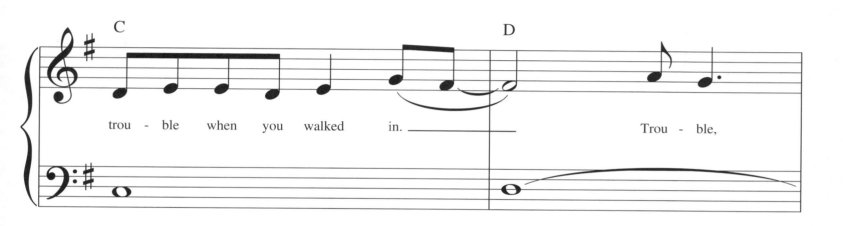

trou - ble when you walked in. _____   Trou - ble,

trou - ble,   trou - ble.   I   knew   you   were

trou - ble when you walked in. _____   Trou - ble,   trou - ble,   trou - ble.

JUST THE WAY YOU ARE

Words and Music by BRUNO MARS,
ARI LEVINE, PHILIP LAWRENCE,
KHARI CAIN and KHALIL WALTON

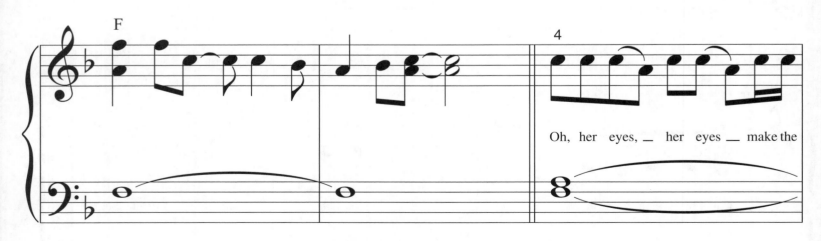

Oh, her eyes, __ her eyes __ make the

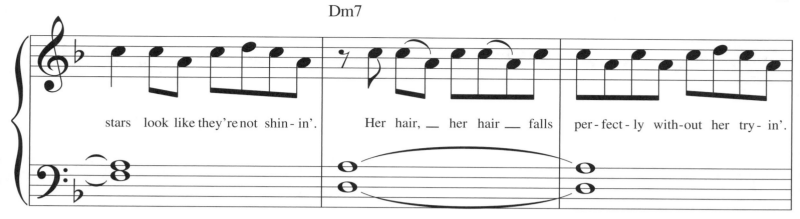

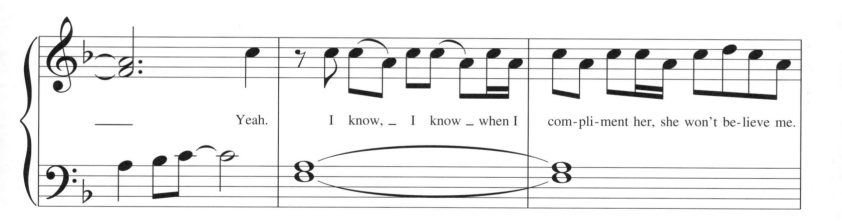

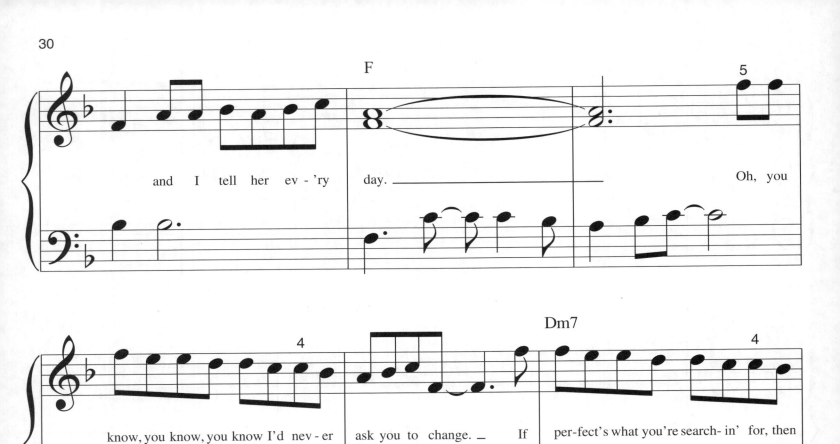

and I tell her ev - 'ry day. _____ Oh, you

know, you know, you know I'd nev - er ask you to change. __ If per-fect's what you're search- in' for, then

just stay the same. __ So __ don't e - ven both - er ask - in' if you look o - kay. You know I'll

say: _____ When I see your face, __

_____ Yeah.

NEED YOU NOW

Words and Music by HILLARY SCOTT,
CHARLES KELLEY, DAVE HAYWOOD
and JOSH KEAR

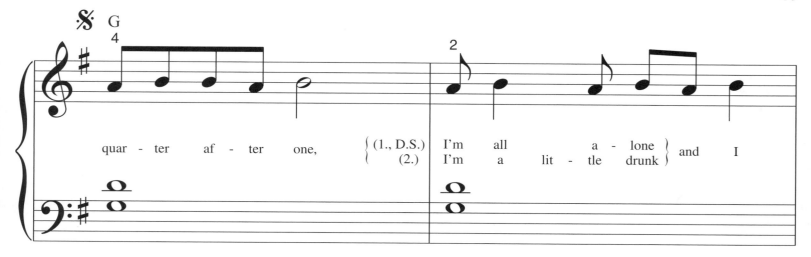

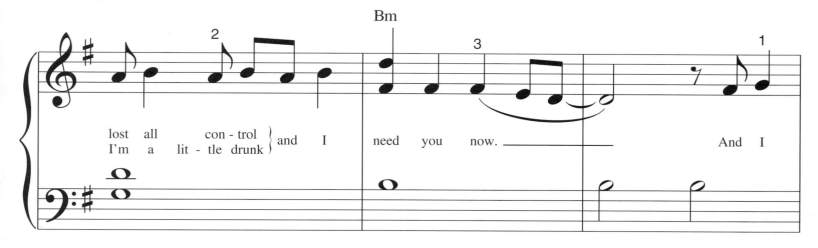

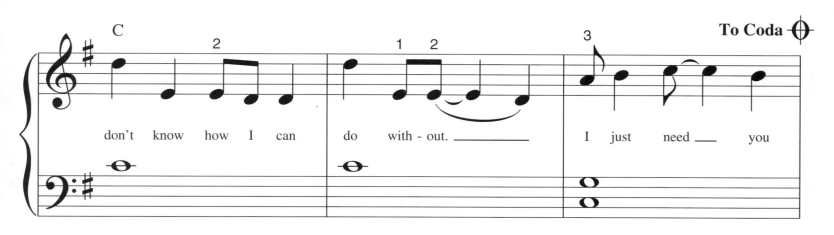

POKER FACE

Words and Music by STEFANI GERMANOTTA
and RedOne

STRONGER
(What Doesn't Kill You)

Words and Music by GREG KURSTIN,
JORGEN ELOFSSON, DAVID GAMSON
and ALEXANDRA TAMPOSI

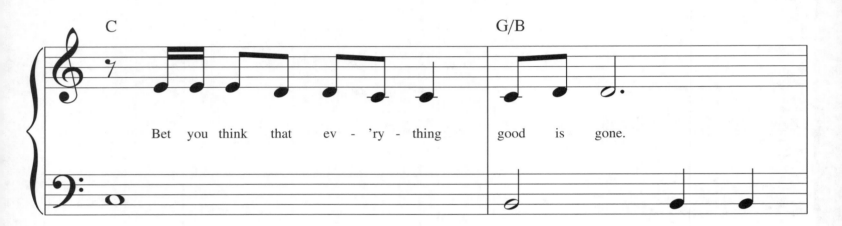

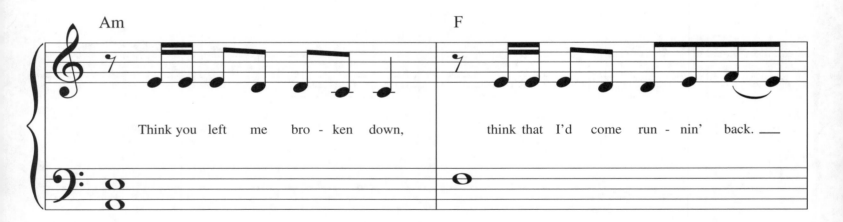

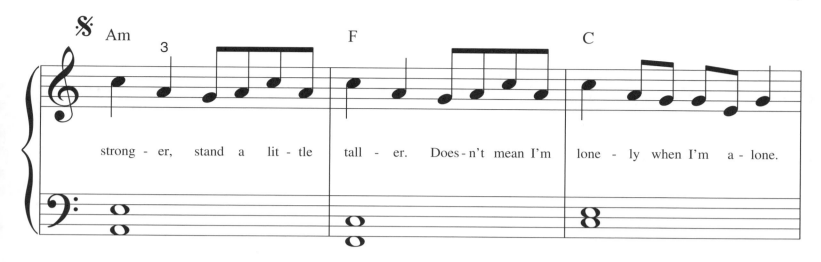

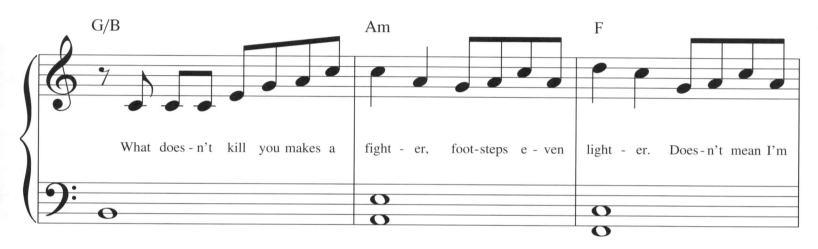

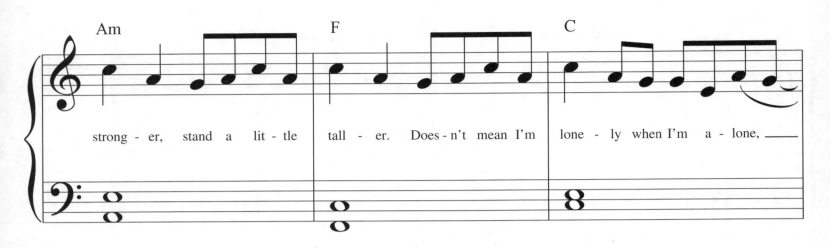

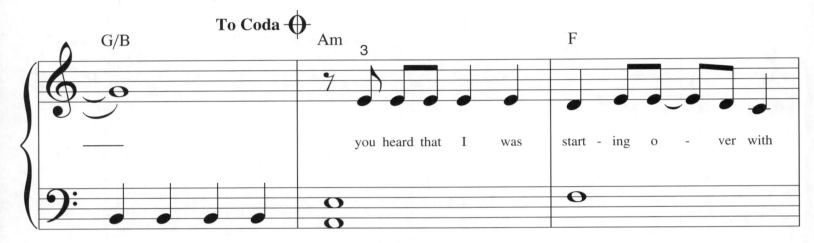

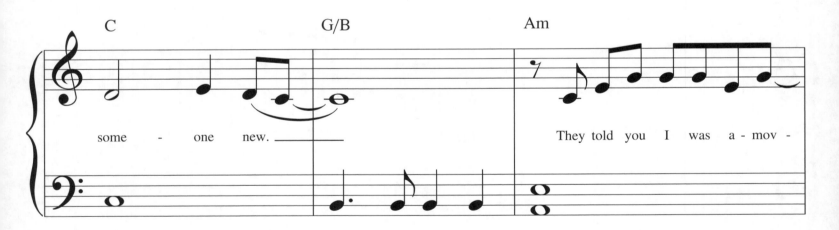

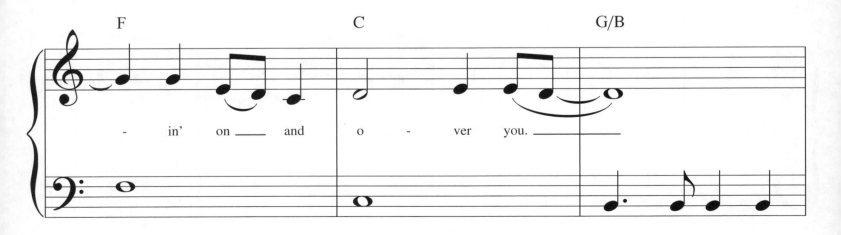

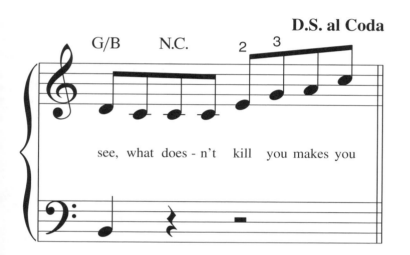

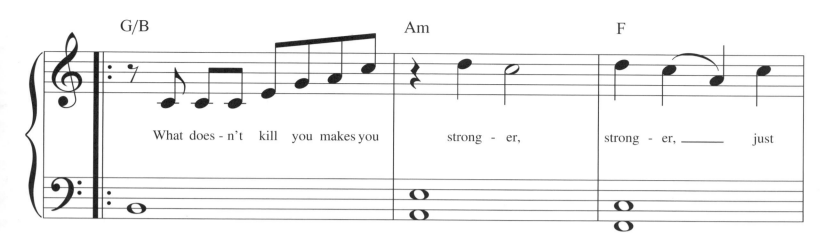

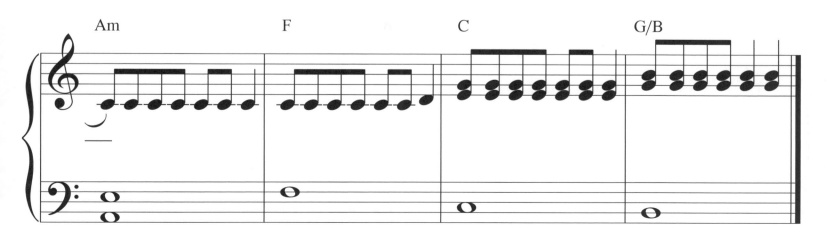

ROLLING IN THE DEEP

Words and Music by ADELE ADKINS
and PAUL EPWORTH

SINGLE LADIES
(Put a Ring on It)

Words and Music by BEYONCE KNOWLES,
THADDIS HARRELL, CHRISTOPHER STEWART
and TERIUS NASH

like it then you should have put a ring on it. Oh, oh, oh, oh, oh, oh, oh, oh, oh, oh, oh, oh. Oh, oh,

G+

oh, oh, oh, oh, oh, oh, oh, oh, oh, oh. If you like it then you should have put a ring on it. If you

G   Gsus   G   G+

like it then you should have put a ring on it. Don't be mad once you see that he want it. If you

1. G   2. G

like it then you should have put a ring on it. I got   like it then you should have put a ring on it. Oh, oh,

oh, oh, oh, oh, oh, oh, oh, oh, oh, oh. Oh, oh, oh, oh, oh, oh, oh, oh,

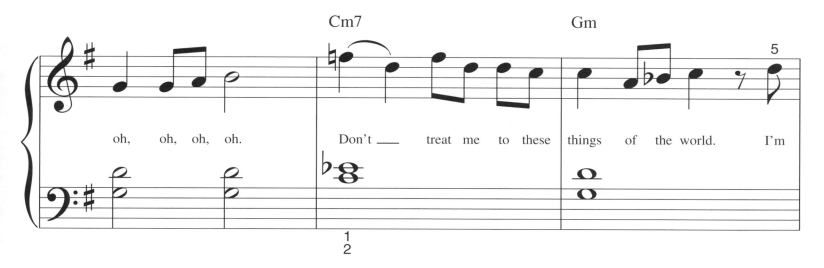

oh, oh, oh, oh. Don't ___ treat me to these things of the world. I'm

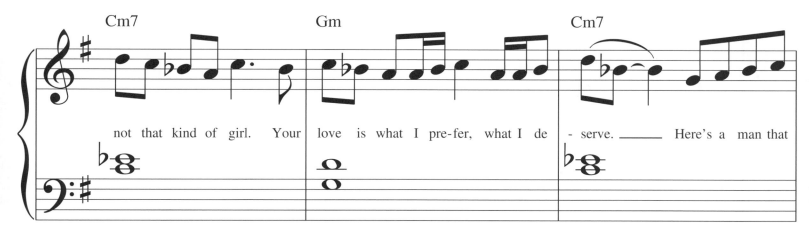

not that kind of girl. Your love is what I pre-fer, what I de - serve. ___ Here's a man that

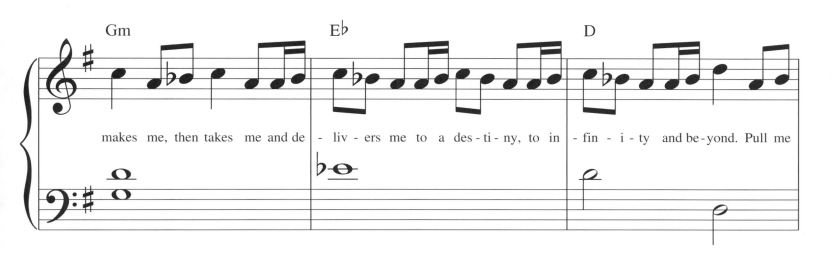

makes me, then takes me and de - liv - ers me to a des - ti - ny, to in - fin - i - ty and be-yond. Pull me

in - to your arms, say I'm the one you want. If you don't, you'll be a - lone and like a

ghost I'll be gone. All the sin - gle la - dies, ___ all the sin - gle la - dies. ___ All the

sin - gle la - dies, ___ all the sin - gle la - dies. ___ All the sin - gle la - dies, ___ all the sin - gle la - dies. ___ All the

sin - gle la - dies, ___ now put your hands up. Oh, oh, oh, oh, oh, oh, oh, oh,

oh, oh, oh, oh. Oh, oh, oh, oh, oh, oh, oh, oh, oh, oh, oh, oh. If you

G   G+   G   Gsus

like it then you should have put a ring on it. If you like it then you should have put a ring on it. Don't be

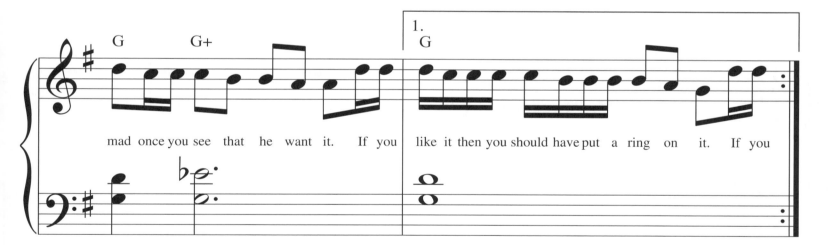

G   G+   1. G

mad once you see that he want it. If you like it then you should have put a ring on it. If you

2. G

like it then you should have put a ring on it.
Oh, oh, oh.

SOME NIGHTS

Words and Music by JEFF BHASKER,
ANDREW DOST, JACK ANTONOFF
and NATE RUESS

Why don't we break the rules al - read - y? I was

nev - er one to be - lieve the hype, __ save that for the black and white. I try

twice as hard and I'm half as liked but here they come a - gain to jack my style.

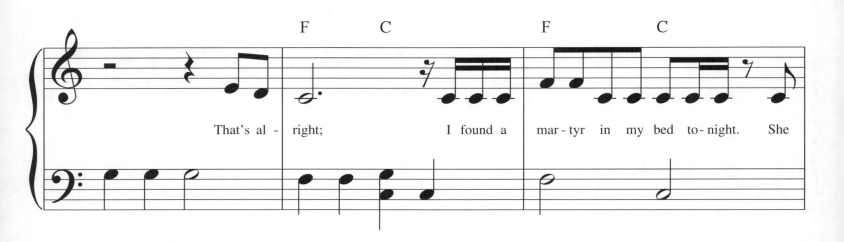

That's al - right; I found a mar - tyr in my bed to - night. She

con that she call "love." ___ And I look in - to my neph - ew's eyes. ___

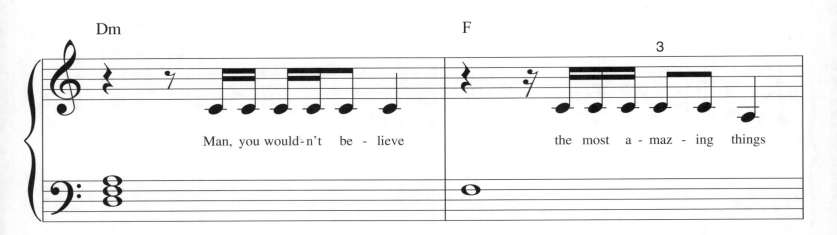

Man, you would-n't be - lieve the most a - maz - ing things

that can come from ___ some ter - ri - ble lies. ___ Oh. ___

Oh.

TEENAGE DREAM

Words and Music by KATY PERRY,
BONNIE McKEE, LUKASZ GOTTWALD,
MAX MARTIN and BENJAMIN LEVIN

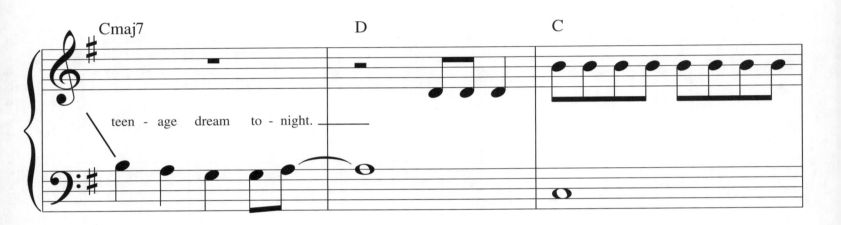

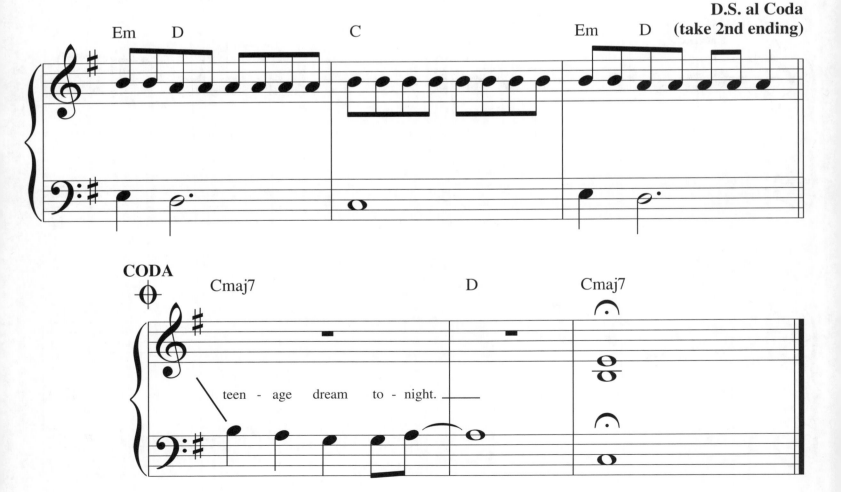

WHAT MAKES YOU BEAUTIFUL

Words and Music by SAVAN KOTECHA,
RAMI YACOUB and CARL FALK

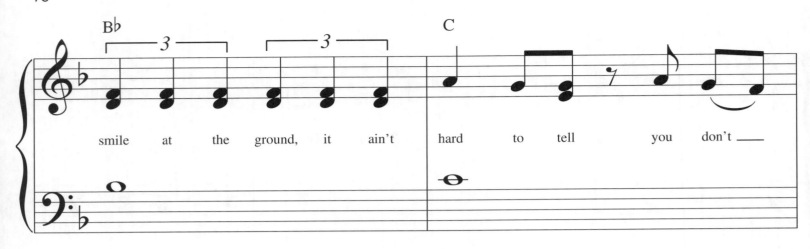

VIVA LA VIDA

Words and Music by GUY BERRYMAN,
JON BUCKLAND, WILL CHAMPION
and CHRIS MARTIN

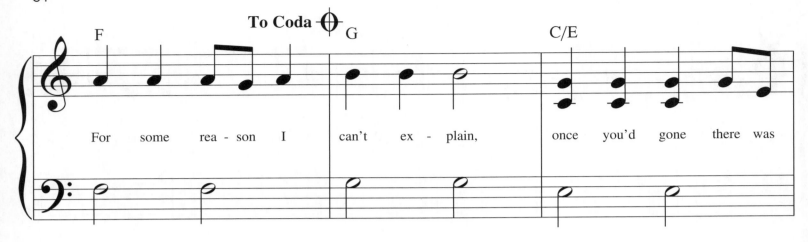

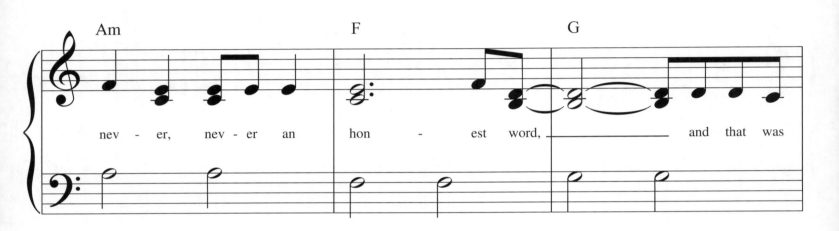

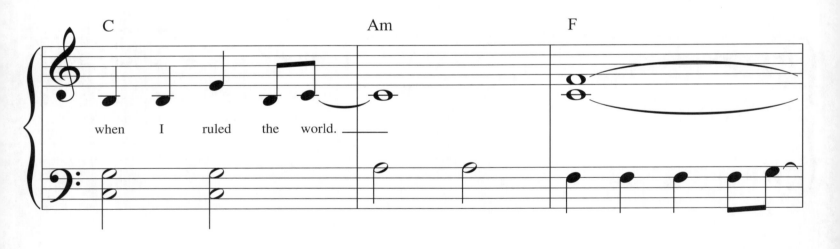

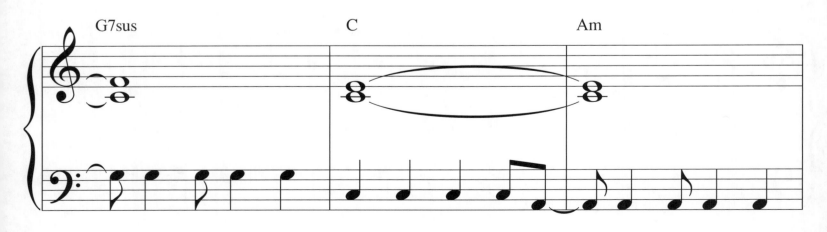

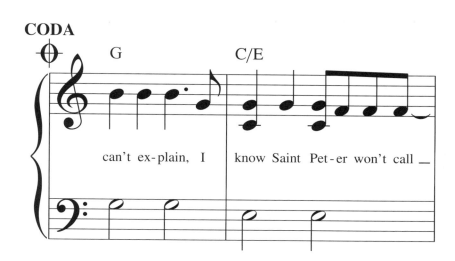

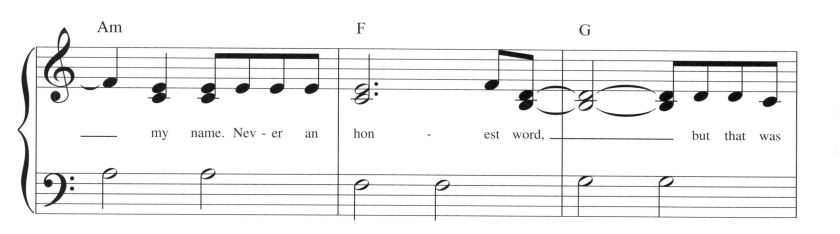

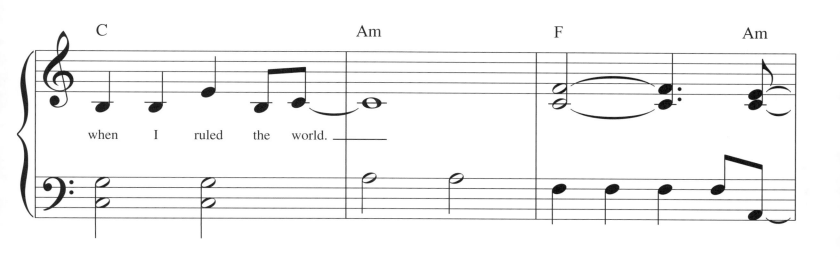

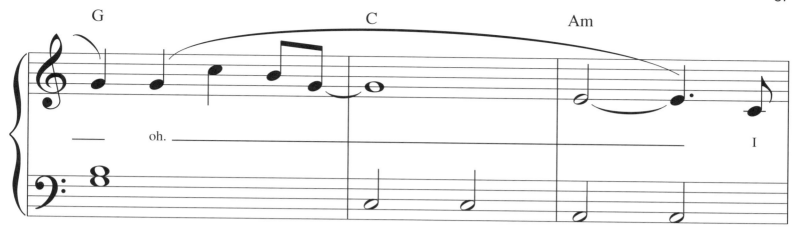

oh. _____ I

hear Je - ru - sa - lem bells _____ a - ring - ing, Ro - man Cath - o - lic

choirs are sing - ing. Be my mir - ror, my sword _____ and shield, ___ my

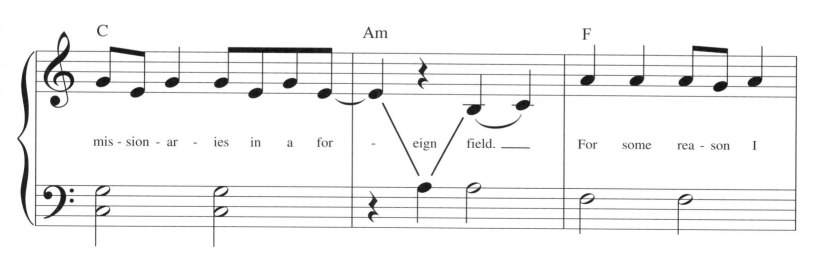

mis - sion - ar - ies in a for - eign field. ___ For some rea - son I

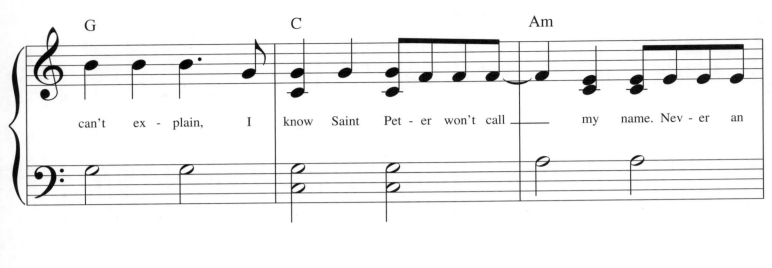

can't ex - plain, I know Saint Pet - er won't call _____ my name. Nev - er an

hon - est word, _____ but that was when I ruled the world. _____

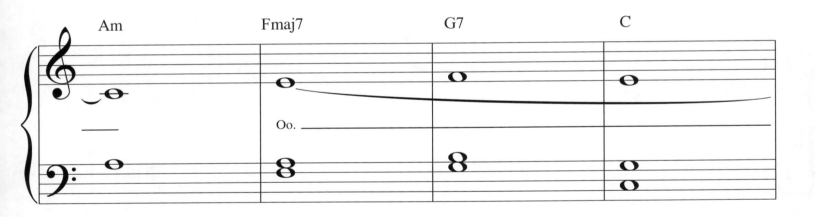

Oo. _____

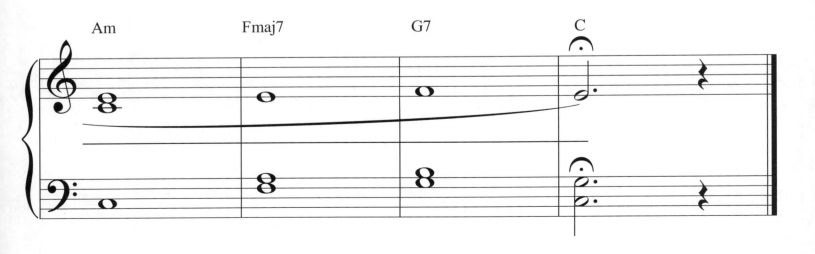